Family Manual For Loved Ones

This is a family manual for your loved ones in the event of your incapacity or death.

It is a subject and project we all would like to avoid, but doing so is a disservice to those we love and leave behind.

Robert H. Scott, Jr.

Copyright, all rights reserved, 2013

CONTENTS

Introduction and General Planning	3
Sample Family Manual	8
Part 1. In the Event of My Incapacitation	8
Part 2. After Death Checklist of Actions	11
Part 3. General Estate Issues and Location of Documents	15
Part 4. Monthly Calendar of Actions	17
Part 5. Miscellaneous	20
Conclusion and Final Thoughts	21
Your Notes and Start on Personal Manual	22

INTRODUCTION AND GENERAL PLANNING

None of us wants to do this. None of us wants to think about our passing and perhaps even more becoming incapacitated before our death leaving a burden on those we love.

That is why wills are put off, powers of attorney are put off and even making a living will and medical directive that will ease the burden of those who have to deal with problems we have not anticipated.

This is not a book only for those in retirement or who have just been diagnosed with a serious illness. It is for anyone of any age who has loved ones and has affairs that they will have to handle on your incapacitation or passing. There is little you can do to show your love more than to anticipate and help them to survive without you.

This book may be helpful even if a manual is not prepared as it will cover subjects to think about and if you are someone charged with taking care of affairs of a friend or family member it may also help you to start a checklist of things you need to check. Of course that is a whole lot easier if there is a manual to help direct you in your search and in performing your duties.

Can we anticipate everything? Likely not. But preparing a manual as suggested in this book is an excellent starting place both for putting your affairs in order and for seeing that those you love can continue on with the least amount of trouble to add to the pain of the loss.

I first heard of preparing a Family Manual from the widow of my former boss at Federated Department Stores. Jack, like me, was a careful planner in all he did. He loved his wife and while they had no children he wanted to make sure that on his passing she knew what she needed to do, where the important papers were located and how to conduct her affairs without him. In any good marriage a husband and wife share the burdens of life as a partnership and over years tend to allocate certain tasks between them. No matter who becomes incapacitated or dies first the other partner has to take up the tasks once done by the other partner. And the problem is even greater when a single person or widow(er) leaves behind children or friends who are charged with the task of sorting out their affairs. That is what this book is about. Setting up a manual to leave for those who have to take up those tasks and hopefully make that burden easier.

I had great respect for my former boss and was impressed when his widow told me what he had done for her. It was a final gift and a loving one. Especially because it is hard to contemplate our own incapacity and death and to face what our survivors will have to deal with. It is always a project for "tomorrow" and sadly it is a tomorrow that often never comes.

While the author is a lawyer this book is not about legal advice for that will differ from state to state and person to person. You will need your own lawyer to help you with the legal aspects of preparing for your incapacity and death. It is not about tax advice for survivors. For that you need to consult your CPA or other tax advisor. What this book IS about is sitting down and sketching out those things that you, or if you are doing this together what you and your spouse, do now that someone other than you will have to deal with should you be in a car accident, suffer a stroke or heart attack or otherwise become incapacitated and eventually on your death.

If you have loved ones this is a task that you should take on as you have the planning of other gifts in lifetime. Only this is a gift that will outlast you and will hopefully bring loving memories to those you leave behind while making their life without you easier.

I initially prepared my own Family Manual for my wife, Sandy, but unfortunately I lost her to cancer the day before Christmas Eve in 2009. After her death I revised the Family Manual for my adult children and it is something that I need to review and update annually.

I will confess that since 2010 I have not done this but it is now on the calendar for January. And that is my first suggestion. Make a note each January to review and revise the manual. It will go out of date. You will move to a new state, you will change brokers or bank accounts. And one of a hundred other things that are routine to you but not to those you leave behind.

But whatever you do, do not put off preparing such a manual. How you do it and what it contains will be very personal to you. While I will provide a sample manual you should take this only as a starting point. Depending on your circumstances you may need to talk to your lawyer, CPA and others about various matters before you finish your manual. But you can start now and I urge you to do so. It is SO easy to put this off to tomorrow.

One important note that I am putting in bold print because it is that important. If you are engaged in litigation or divorce or have other personal circumstances which requires that a manual of this nature be kept confidential then you may want to consult with your attorney before starting a manual and be guided by your attorney's advice as to whether to prepare this manual at all or if you do where it should be kept. Your attorney may be able to keep this for you as a confidential document and if so take their advice as to how to handle the matter.

Subject to the caveat in the paragraph above, how do you start? I suggest you skim through the sample manual below and get an idea of the items I have covered in my own manual and then sketch out your own Family Manual. You can create other parts than I have created and likely will. For example, I do not have a business to pass on to my children but if you do you will need to discuss this in detail for them. And that is just an example. You may own rental or farm property or have other items that need specific attention.

Doing this will also do more for you than just prepare your survivors to deal with your incapacitation or death. It will force you to think through a number of difficult subjects like your funeral arrangements, how you feel about being hospitalized and what actions those in your family should or should not take about your condition. It will require you to organize you records and finances.

It is hoped that you are comfortable using a computer and that you can write your own manual on the computer. But if not then a handwritten manual will work just as well. In fact you will probably want to start on paper even if later preparing this document on your computer.

You will find things you forget, especially as you go through a year, and things come up you did not remember to include. So take the first year as a "test run" adding things as you go along.

You may want to keep a pad for each section and make notes in each of these as you think of things. Those pads can serve as your temporary manual should something happen before you are able to finish the manual. And of course it is of no use whatsoever if your family does not know where it is located! You do not have to share all the details of the manual if you do not want to and probably should not do so in many cases. It is hard enough for them to deal with when you are no longer in control or have passed on. I had many a tear in my eye when redoing mine that I had prepared for my wife of over 43 years after her passing. I knew I had to do it for my children but had never thought I would be rewriting it after her passing. Conditions change and so must the manual you prepare.

I was struck by the love and care that my former boss left for his wife in doing this for her. And I know how much she appreciated what he had done and how much easier it made the burden of handling their affairs once she had to take up the task. I only hope that my own manual does the same for my children and that yours will make life easier and better for those you love and leave behind.

I wish you well in preparing your manual and only urge you not to delay. You may have to leave certain matters open while you think them through or consult with others. If you have not prepared a Durable Power of Attorney, or a Living Will or a Last Will and Testament these are tasks you need to consult your personal attorney about and it will entail making a number of decisions you probably would rather not think about. But failing to do so is frankly selfish and hopefully if you have read this far in the book you will know that you should not delay. The old Latin phrase *carpe diem* translates as "live for today". That applies to preparing your manual for survivors. Today is the day to start and if you do I think you will be surprised how quickly you will handle most of this.

In this sample manual below in bold italics are items not to be included in the manual but which will help explain what you need to think about in its preparation. This sample is written for one person but it could be written for spouses together. Your personal situation will dictate how you handle this as well as all the items to include. Items in parentheses ( ) are for you to delete and insert your own material.

After its preparation you may wish to leave copies of this manual with your lawyer and your tax advisor and perhaps others who you think will be in position to be sure your survivors have a copy. Also your survivors should know where you keep this. And of course as you make changes you will need to substitute copies of the revision for the ones out of date. Being careful about any sensitive information, if you have put your manual on computer you can save it to the cloud and e mail it to your family members. But do be careful not to have included information which if intercepted could result in identity theft or other problems. So no social security numbers, no computer passwords and no account numbers should be included. And because of security you may not want to take advantage of these ways to share your manual. That is a personal decision.

A final important note:

You do not have to fill in all the information that is in the sample manual. Depending on your circumstance, your advisors may feel you should merely reference contacting them about details. This is particularly true if you are involved in litigation, complicated business transactions or any one of a number of other situations beyond the scope of this book. But even in these cases a simple manual covering items that you can cover and with reference to your advisors for other matters should still be of great help to those called upon to manage or wrap up your affairs.

FAMILY MANUAL FOR (Insert name)

Last Revised: (Insert date)

Important Notes:

Items mentioned in this manual will change, so consult the latest version of this manual. Even that may be out of date so consider this manual as a guideline not a list of fixed rules.

This manual is for my survivors in the hopes that it will help them in a difficult time to deal with all the things that must be handled to take care of or wrap up my affairs and to be sure my wishes are carried out. It is prepared in love as a final gift and I can only hope I have anticipated many if not all of the things you will face in the event of my incapacitation and death.

A copy of this manual is (insert here where the original is located and if you have left copies with your attorney, tax advisor or others).

This manual is divided into parts and there may be overlaps between them. The first section is designed to guide you through the initial stages of steps to be taken in the event of my illness and incapacitation. Some items may turn out to be unnecessary or need to be done differently. But hopefully this will help.

Part 1. In the Event of My Incapacitation

Probably more than death we fear illness or accident that leaves us unable to conduct our own affairs. We have all known someone in this situation and it can strike us at any age or can be simply the result of aging. Whatever the circumstance it leaves a burden on the loved ones having to deal not only with certain or likely loss of their loved one temporarily or permanently but requires someone to carry on their affairs.

Not anticipating the event can leave a major burden on loved ones. Hospitals and doctors today try to get patients to sign living wills and medical directives or whatever they may be called in a particular state to deal with this prior to incapacity. That is fine if you are still in condition to do this. It is far better to do this before the need arises.

Step one in this manual is therefor to tell your survivors what to do in the event of incapacity.

1. **Medical Directive and Living Will**. I have prepared the documents that express my wishes as to what I want done in the event I am unable to express my wishes as to my medical care. A copy has been left with (insert here where this can be found such as with your attorney, safe deposit box, a file in your office, hopefully you have already given a copy to your survivors, your doctor, the hospital likely to be patient, or others where this will be quickly accessible in case of need. The author keeps one in the trunk of his car. You may be tempted to repeat here what is in these documents but should not do so as it might muddy the waters later if there is any conflict with your medical directive or living will. Let those documents speak for themselves.)

2. **Durable Power of Attorney**. I have prepared a Durable Power of Attorney which names those who are to act in my stead while I am incapacitated. (This is a document that should be prepared for you by a lawyer as every State differs as to the legal requirements. A durable power differs from a non durable power of attorney in that the latter does not survive your incapacity but a durable power does. That is important. I suggest that you have this power come into effect only under certain conditions and not from the date of its execution. For example, in the event you are unable for any reason to handle your affairs and only for the period you are incapacitated. Unfortunately there are horror stories of powers of attorney given to loved ones or friends who have abused that power and when someone has recovered discovers that they have been taken advantage of by those they trusted. You must have absolute faith in those you name to act for you and if you do not then you need to talk to your lawyer how best to handle this.)

3. **Inter Vivos Trust**. (Insert here whether or not you have an Inter Vivos (Living) Trust. This can be relatively simple or very complicated and needs the help of an attorney and likely a tax advisor. The concept is to put property you own in trust with you as the creator/settlor and for you to act as your own trustee during your lifetime while you are capable of acting on your own behalf. State law will govern this document and you will need to think it through carefully to be sure that it accomplishes what you wish. While a Durable Power of Attorney will substitute in many cases this trust will give you certain protections that the Durable Power will not. It is beyond the purpose of this book to write in detail about an Inter Vivos Trust but it is something anyone with property of substance should consider with their attorney.)

4. **Miscellaneous:** (Depending on your circumstances there may be matters you need to insert here such as what happens to a business you own, property you own that needs care, or any of a hundred other items including what to do about a pet in event you are incapacitated temporarily or permanently and on your passing.)

Part 2. After Death Checklist of Actions

Things to do as soon as possible after death:

1. **Funeral Arrangements**: (If you have preplanned your funeral here you need to indicate details and direct your survivors where to go and what to do. If you have not preplanned then you need to indicate here your desires as to how your funeral is to be handled. If covered in your will you should note that and not repeat here.)

2. **You will need death certificates:** These are needed for a variety of reasons. Initially at least 10 should be ordered since it takes time to get them. Keep at least one in the master file of estate matters.

3. **Price of Securities**: (If you own stocks or bonds outside of a 401(k), IRA or other tax deferred account then include this item. If not then indicate that here.) Buy several copies of the Wall Street Journal that has stock prices listed for the date of death - will be the paper day after death but be careful of weekends and make sure prices in the paper are as of date of death or if death occurs on a weekend or holiday the last business day before. In some cases you may have option of electing a later valuation date and if so you will need papers for that date as well. Accountant can guide you on this matter. In event of assets entitled to step up in basis -tax cost- of stocks you will need this to value any stocks later sold. This applies only to individual securities and not IRA or stocks held in other tax deferred accounts such as 401(k). As of 2012 brokers are required to include and step up values on death but you will need to contact them to be sure they take steps to do this. Not doing so could be very costly to you in taxes.

Items that should be done shortly after funeral arrangements made:

4. **Set up a banker's box and create file folders** for estate work. Correspondence. Probate. Final Expenses. Estate Tax. Income Tax. Appraisals. Transfer of Ownership. Stock Valuations (Wall Street Journal),

Business Affairs (or multiples of these if several businesses to consider). Miscellaneous. These are good files to start with. At end of the process store this box for future reference.

5. **Decide on attorney to use and also accountant**. Ask them before appointment what papers they want to have you bring them. You will want to discuss with attorney waiving any fees you might be entitled to as executor especially if you are to receive the estate since an executor fee is usually income taxable while a distribution is not. If waiver is done it should be completed prior to taking office. You should show both attorney and accountant this manual if they do not already have a copy. Attorney will need original of wills and trusts as well as general description of real and personal property. Printing out from computer spreadsheets listing securities and budgets will be helpful as will latest copies of tax returns and brokerage and bank statements.

6. **Take a two year calendar with you to all meetings**. Be prepared to record dates when steps need to be taken e.g., final income tax return, estate tax return, if any, appraisal of property, whether needed for estate tax or not to establish FMV on date of death of items that might later be sold at a profit. Will lessen any capital gains otherwise payable.

Next steps likely will be:

7. **Attorney will file the will for probate and obtain letters for executor.** Your attorney will outline what steps need to be taken to list property and to transfer property from joint or POD/TOD, pay or transfer on death, into new names. Accountant will give dates when various returns are needed and can help in deciding how to handle IRA accounts. If you have IRA or 401(k) accounts looking into beneficiaries and deciding how best to handle these accounts should start early. Also when transferred, new beneficiaries needed for those taking over these accounts.

8. **Early item to attend to will be notifying Social Security of the death**. This is easiest to do by visiting the office and taking copy of social security card with you. They will then cut off any social security payments being made and arrange for the small death benefit. Also need to check with insurance company regarding coverage for house and car in event of death of last to survive. You may need to wait on obtaining death certificate.

9. **As soon as you have the death certificates** you can begin to distribute these to insurance companies for death benefits, POD/TOD,(Pay or transfer on Death, and joint asset accounts to put in name of beneficiary/joint tenant e.g., bank accounts, brokerage accounts that are in POD/TOD, automobiles, real estate deeds in joint name.

10. **Start lists of those items that transfer outside of probate** e.g., joint accounts, POD/TOD accounts and check these off as transfer is made. Then list those items that are included in estate subject to probate. If because of advance planning those items in the probate estate will not be much this can usually allow for a short form of probate. If there is an Inter Vivos Trust then review of this should take place shortly after death to see who the successor trustee is and for them to begin to take steps as dictated by that trust and required by law.

11. **Create checklist for all actions needed after consulting with attorney and accountant.** Be sure to note any critical dates. Once outline of how things will be distributed consider any changes you need to make in beneficiaries of your IRA, POD/TOD accounts etc. Also any changes in your own estate planning that may be indicated. Need to have mail forwarded to executor. Various accounts need to be cancelled after any payments due are made. This would include credit cards and any items automatically charged there or to bank account e.g., health insurance, satellite coverage, etc. Bills should guide you in the process. If there are substantial debts outstanding you likely will need an attorney's advice on how to handle these matters. You may find substantial medical bills that keep rolling in long after incapacity or death that need to be considered. And you need to know after what period debts can no longer be claimed against an estate.

12. **Internet passwords and e bills.** *(I do not believe people should use e bills as is constantly being urged these days as a "green" alternative to paper. Without a bill in the mail those who are responsible to step in will not in many cases know what accounts are out there they have to deal with. Unfortunately the most "green" that this serves is the companies who save money not mailing you bills. That can turn very "red" very quickly if you are incapacitated or die and those handing your affairs do not know about these bills until too late. Unfortunately companies are getting more aggressive and Sprint recently sent a notice they would automatically start you on e billing unless you called and told them otherwise – the author did that!)* Because of e billing you need to know accounts where only bills you will see come via e billing. You may have to call those companies and get this changed and meanwhile here is where you can find a list of all of my on line accounts, user names and passwords you will need to address my accounts and take care of closing them after taking any steps needed (tell where this can be found – probably better than putting the information here as this is sensitive information).

Part 3. General Estate Issues and Location of Documents

1. **Safe deposit box:** (list and tell where keys may be found and who has access. If you do not have a safe deposit box that should be noted. If you have a safe tell where it is and give the combination or tell where it may be found).

2. **Location of major documents not listed below:** (Where your will is located and if your state (and will) allows you to designate specific personal property to go to specified persons in separate writing indicate whether you have done that and if so where it is located. List if you have a medical directive, durable power of attorney, living trust (Inter Vivos) or other such important documents and where they can be located. For the medical directive and durable power of attorney at least one copy should be readily available as needed.)

3. **Bank accounts, CD's and other similar assets:** (list here and give location of checkbooks, passbooks, etc. Because sensitive you should give location and not include here account numbers. If you have securities not held by your broker list those and where the certificates may be found). If you have mortgages, car loans or other indebtedness be sure to list the details and contacts.

4. **Brokerage accounts:** (list accounts, where records are kept and the name and phone number of contacts but do not include account numbers in your manual).

5. **Insurance policies: life, health, auto, homeowner etc:** (All need to be listed along with where documents are located, broker to contact or any other information needed to keep in force, cancel, collect on or modify depending on whether dealing with incapacity or death).

6. **Credit Cards:** (list along with where they are located and any specific information about them, if any, but do not include numbers in your manual).

7. **Bills, Miscellaneous and Tax Records**: (Where the current records are kept and back year's records and supporting documents).

8. **Veterans Rights and Funeral Arrangement**: (Here include any special items that may apply to a Veteran such as burial in national cemetery, formalities at funeral as well as the same information for non veterans and if that is included in will be sure to reference here but do not repeat as that may cause confusion if differs from what is included in your will).

9. **Miscellaneous:** (Your personal situation is likely to include any number of items the author has not thought of or considered but which will be obvious to you. This is a place to list some of these items.)

Part 4. Monthly Calendar of Actions

Every Month

(These actions are needed monthly, every month)

Listed here are actions that are needed every month and then by month specific items. (Included below are some of the items that apply to nearly everyone but you need to use your own list and going through your checkbook and calendar for the last year or two will be a good place to start to build this important item for those having to take over and manage your affairs).

1. Verify that insurance premiums are paid when due, same with all utility bills, mortgage payments, car loans, etc. If paid from checking automatically be sure there are sufficient funds in the account not to be in default.

2. Check all credit cards to see when payments are due and if e bills be sure you know what is due and if necessary call the companies to get current amounts that are due.

3. When bank and brokerage statements are due during the month.

4. (Add items to do regularly, like changing oil in car, when and how to handle car registration and if safety check is needed list that along with the steps and places to go to accomplish this as needed. If your state requires filing personal property or other tax statements detail when and how this is to be done).

January

15th Estimated tax payment for the 4th installment (US and State) are due.

February

W-2 and 1099 Tax records should be received and filed. REIT ownership will require waiting for broker corrected 1099 forms middle of March before doing taxes.

March

Check any mandatory IRA or other tax deferred distributions from the prior year (age 69 and over) and be sure to make withdrawals to avoid stiff and unnecessary penalties.

April

US and State tax returns (or extensions) are due along with first quarterly estimated tax on 15th. Or extensions need to be filed.

May

June

15th Second Quarterly Estimated Taxes (US and State) are due.

July

August

September

15th Third Quarterly Estimated Tax payment (US and State) are due.

October

November

December

Part 5: Miscellaneous

1. **Computer passwords are kept:** (insert here where these are kept along with user names and passwords).

2. (If you have a pension plan or other similar plan be sure to list and describe actions needed if incapacitated and then on death. Same with any disability or other insurance (like AFLAC) you may have).

3. (For anyone on or near Social Security and/or Medicare list items needed to know).

4. (Any other items that you need to include. If you have a business or own rental property or farm land you may need to add special sections to deal with these issues).

Conclusion and Final Thoughts

If you have gotten this far my congratulations. It has not been an easy task for you and I know that. But keep remembering how important it is for you to prepare this manual and to update it. In addition to helping those you leave behind, temporarily or permanently, it will also help you to organize your affairs.

There are many matters not covered above. Chief among these are situations involving divorce, litigation pending and business affairs. These are just too complex to try to cover in the suggested manual but if these, or other matters, affect you and your loved ones then you will need to include sections dealing with those matters.

I thought it a very loving act for my former boss to have done this for his wife and I hope that passing this on to you will help you leave behind a special legacy that will be appreciated by your loved ones and give them a special memory of you as they adjust to a life without you.

Hopefully this is a manual that will not be needed for many years and will require many revisions. But none of us can count on that. Whatever you do don't delay and put this task off for another day. Often that day never comes.

Below you will find blank pages that you may find useful in sketching out your own family manual. It is suggested you do this in pencil for revisions are nearly certain as you will think of things or change your mind about specific items.

My Personal Manual – Notes to Start

Part 1. In the Event of My Incapacitation:

Put here if you do or do not have a durable power of attorney, living will and details on your doctors, medications, hospital of choice as well as any instructions what to do at your residence both with mail, pets, bills, etc. If you have an attorney, CPA, etc. list them here along with their contact information. If you have an inter vivos trust note that as well as any investment advisor or broker you use. Anything that needs to be attended to while you are incapacitated should be listed here.

My Personal Manual – Notes to Start

Part 2. After Death Checklist of Actions

Items to Attend To Immediately:

Here include any prearranged funeral arrangements, choice of funeral home and if included in your will reference to your will, quoting exactly, any instructions in your will. Do not elaborate if in your will as this could cause confusion and delay. Best if you merely refer to it and indicate where it may be found. If you want DNA samples taken before burial or cremation this is place to add that. It could be helpful to your family later.

My Personal Manual – Notes to Start

Part 2. After Death Checklist of Actions

Death Certificates: Here include any information on where and how to obtain these recommending at least ten of them be obtained as soon as possible as they are needed for TOD or POD (Transfer or Pay on Death) accounts, transfer of automobile titles, collecting on insurance and many other needs. Where possible provide copies and keep originals. But often originals are required. Sometimes they will be returned especially if you ask for return.

My Personal Manual – Notes to Start

Part 2. After Death Checklist of Actions

Price of Securities: If you own securities on your death it is a good idea for those handling your affairs to get copies of Wall Street Journal or Investor Business Daily for the last trading day on or before your date of death as these values are likely to be used to step up the value of these securities for tax purposes. Today on the internet through Yahoo Finance you may be able to find these but having paper copy is valuable. Your broker should step these up in value, if appropriate, but it is likely those managing your estate will have to work with them to make sure this is done properly so having these values handy and in paper form will help. There are circumstances where a date later may be elected and if that is the case (the tax advisor they use can advise them) then paper for that date should be saved as well.

My Personal Manual – Notes to Start

Part 2. After Death Checklist of Actions

Next Steps: See the manual above and make notes here that may be useful to those managing your estate. A number of items are included above so more than one page is provided here for your use.

My Personal Manual – Notes to Start

Part 2. After Death Checklist of Actions

Next Steps: See the manual above and make notes here that may be useful to those managing your estate. A number of items are included above so more than one page is provided here for your use.

My Personal Manual – Notes to Start

Part 2. After Death Checklist of Actions

Next Steps: See the manual above and make notes here that may be useful to those managing your estate. A number of items are included above so more than one page is provided here for your use.

My Personal Manual – Notes to Start

Part 2. After Death Checklist of Actions

Next Steps: See the manual above and make notes here that may be useful to those managing your estate. A number of items are included above so more than one page is provided here for your use.

My Personal Manual – Notes to Start

Part 3. General Estate Issues and Location of Documents

As with Part 2 there are a number of items to include here so refer back to the Manual and tailor these to your personal situation. Again, a number of pages are included here for your convenience.

My Personal Manual – Notes to Start

Part 3. General Estate Issues and Location of Documents

As with Part 2 there are a number of items to include here so refer back to the Manual and tailor these to your personal situation. Again, a number of pages are included here for your convenience.

My Personal Manual – Notes to Start

Part 3. General Estate Issues and Location of Documents

As with Part 2 there are a number of items to include here so refer back to the Manual and tailor these to your personal situation. Again, a number of pages are included here for your convenience.

My Personal Manual – Notes to Start

Part 3. General Estate Issues and Location of Documents

As with Part 2 there are a number of items to include here so refer back to the Manual and tailor these to your personal situation. Again, a number of pages are included here for your convenience.

My Personal Manual – Notes to Start

Part 4. Monthly Calendar of Actions

Go through your calendar, your checkbook and other information and detail those items which in event of your incapacity or death need to be done by those handling your affairs. Items for every month such as utility bills, mail, appointments to change or cancel, should be listed here along with any information needed to act in your place. Then for each month that may have special items such as paying taxes, insurance renewals add those by month.

Items for every month:

January

February

March

April

May

June

July

August

September

October

November

December

My Personal Manual – Notes to Start

Part 5: Miscellaneous

There are items in the manual to consider including here. But everyone will have different needs and there will be things not considered in this manual that you will think of and want to include here. Again, a couple of pages are included for your use.

My Personal Manual – Notes to Start

Part 5: Miscellaneous

There are items in the manual to consider including here. But everyone will have different needs and there will be things not considered in this manual that you will think of and want to include here. Again, a couple of pages are included for your use.

My Personal Manual – Notes to Start

Part 5: Miscellaneous

There are items in the manual to consider including here. But everyone will have different needs and there will be things not considered in this manual that you will think of and want to include here. Again, a couple of pages are included for your use.

www.ingramcontent.com/pod-product-compliance
Lightning Source LLC
Chambersburg PA
CBHW081803170526
45167CB00008B/3307